The Balanced Spiritual Diet: a 30-Day Challenge

A Month-long Devotional Journey to Encourage, Edify
and Equip the Spiritually Hungry

Published by:
Live With Purpose Publishing
3113 Main St., Suite A5, Conestoga, PA 17516
www.livewithpurposecoaching.com

ISBN# 978-1508817154
Copyright © 2015
Printed in the United States of America

Scripture quotations taken from the Holy Bible, New International Version®. Copyright © 1973, 1978, 1984 Biblica. Used by permission of Zondervan. All rights reserved. All Scripture quotations unless indicated otherwise are taken from the New International Version® of the Holy Bible.

Acknowledgements

- *Compiled and edited by Joe D'Orsie*
- *Design by Peter Stevenson*

Primarily, we thank God for writing his laws on our hearts. Thanks also to everyone who made this devotional possible! Thanks to each contributor for the time and devotion they put into their work and thanks to everyone that was involved with the review and publishing process. A special thanks to our Art Director, Peter Stevenson, for making it look pretty.

Table of Contents

The Balanced Spiritual Diet: a 30-Day Challenge
A Month-long Devotional Journey to Encourage, Edify and Equip the
Spiritually Hungry

Introduction

I've heard it said that the #1 criterion for hosting the Holy Spirit *well*, whether it's personally, as a church congregation, or as a region or movement, is hunger. How hungry are you for God and His ways? How utterly famished are you for His presence? How dependent on His Holy Spirit are you? These questions serve as a good check in how it is that you're relating to God and entertaining His Holy Spirit in your life. Your level of hunger will always dictate your level of intimacy with God and likewise the level of good fruit you're able to bear.

*"Like newborn babies, crave pure spiritual milk, so that by it you may grow up in your salvation, now that you have tasted that the Lord is good." – **1st Peter 2:2-3***

'**Spiritual Hunger**' has become our main criterion for putting together a devotional that takes aim at a balanced spiritual diet purposed to address your hunger for His ways while targeting a state of perpetual desire. Tasting that the Lord is, in fact good, should drive this yearning for more of the spiritual essentials that keep you in His will. Each entry from our team, our pastors and our friends are angled toward finding a God-centered hunger and quenching it with nothing short of His presence, His word and His ways. This "sampler platter" of biblical principles collected in the form of a month-long daily devotional should satisfy your spiritual appetite, yet instigate your craving for more.

Our response to the question of 'how hungry are you?' in a time and season set apart by its urgency should be: EXTREMELY. We are EXTREMELY hungry for His ways, presence and spirit. Our prayer is that you attain or maintain this spiritual extremity with the help and encouragement of the words that follow.

Here's to your spiritual health!

"I am the Lord your God, who brought you up out of Egypt. Open wide your mouth and I will fill it." – Psalm 81:10

Joe D'Orsie
Communications & Spiritual Life Counsel
Live With Purpose Coaching, LLC

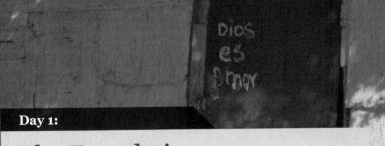

The Foundation

As listed in Hebrews, there are certain 'essentials' to being established in the truth and the salvation of the Lord. Think of 'salvation' in complete terms, not just exiting earth and entering Heaven. In the New Testament context, Salvation, or Soteria in Greek, more wholly means deliverance, preservation, safety, redemption and blessing. Salvation is a place of peace and confidence where fear and worry does not reside and it is a spiritual climate that can be applied here and now. These elements are foundational to our diets but are basic in the sense that they shouldn't be all we eat. The Hebrews 6 metaphor compares milk and meat; milk being necessary for infants while meat is required to preserve and maintain the mature person. Milk was necessary in the nourishment of the new or 'immature' believer but meat is part of the balanced diet for the growing and developing Christian.

1 Corinthians 3 - Milk and solid food

Hebrews 6:1-2 provides us with the nourishment we need to grow up into the "full stature of Christ." It lists six basic tenets of the Christian life that should serve as a foundation for the spirit-filled person:

1. *Repentance*
2. *Faith toward God*
3. *Baptism*
4. *Laying on of Hands*
5. *Resurrection of the Dead*
6. *Eternal Judgment*

"Therefore, let us go on toward perfection (or maturity) leaving behind the basic teaching about Christ, and not laying again the foundation: repentance from dead works[1] and faith toward God[2], instruction about baptisms[3], laying on of hands[4], resurrection of the dead[5], and eternal judgment[6]." **Hebrews 6:1-2 NRSV**

Prayer: Lord, establish me and ground me in the bedrock of your ways so that I can grow and mature from the firmest of foundations. Thank you for both milk and solid food and prescribe to me to a diet that yields good spiritual fruit.

Note: You'll find each foundational essential [numbered above, from the Hebrews text] in succession throughout the Devotional – they're starred * for your convenience.

by **Joe D'Orsie**

Communications & Spiritual Life Counsel
Live With Purpose Coaching, LLC

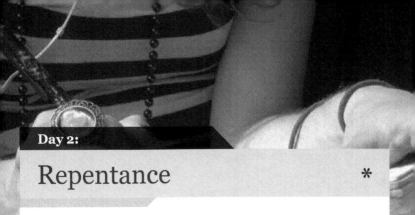

Day 2:

Repentance *

"...if my people, who are called by my name, will humble themselves and pray and seek my face and turn from their wicked ways, then I will hear from heaven, and I will forgive their sin and will heal their land." **2nd Chronicles 7:14**

Repentance is a precondition to freedom, revival and an awakening (notice that the 2nd Chronicles verse is very much addressed to a corporate "people"). IF my people repent [and separate themselves from wickedness] then I'll hear, forgive and heal.' Repentance does not have to carry the negative aura that many times turns people off; it's a problem when repentance is synonymous with condemnation or legalism like it has at times become in the American church. Besides, God's kindness is intended to lead us to repentance.

"Or do you show contempt for the riches of his kindness, forbearance and patience, not realizing that God's kindness is intended to lead you to repentance?" **Romans 2:4**

Elijah to John the Baptist, to Jesus' 12 disciples carried the message of repentance, baptism and renewal;

repentance usually being the first order of business in the transformation of the person as a result of the good news of the Gospel. The act of repentance, or its process, is essential in coming to know God.

"Until we receive the fullness of Christ, we're living in a **process of repentance**." – Adam Bower

-Repentance can even involve intercession for nations, groups and governments just as much as it can involve a personal request for reconciliation. Daniel repented on behalf of his people in **Daniel 9**, not because he was guilty of their sins, but because he chose to represent them through intercession. He desired that they turn from wickedness, which is why he took responsibility for their iniquity.

*"...we have sinned and done wrong. We have been wicked and have rebelled; we have turned away from your commands and laws. 6 We have not listened to your servants the prophets, who spoke in your name to our kings, our princes and our ancestors, and to all the people of the land." **(Daniel 9: 5-6)***

Prayer: 1) Repent for anything personally as it applies to your relationship with the Lord and others. Ask God to scan your heart for areas of disobedience that you've not been aware of. Ask him to wash you clean.

2) Intercede on behalf of the sins of your land, community, municipality, etc. Ask Holy Spirit to reveal specific areas where you're able to cry out to God for patience, favor and forgiveness in the midst of rebellion and disobedience.

"Or do you show contempt for the riches of his kindness, forbearance and patience, not realizing that God's kindness is intended to lead you to repentance?" **Romans 2:4**

by **Joe D'Orsie**
Communications & Spiritual Life Counsel
Live With Purpose Coaching, LLC

Day 3:

Forgiveness - Part I

When you think about it, much hurt has been caused in our world. You might think of the Holocaust or other large-scale tragedies. Maybe you think about those being persecuted around the globe or even the local teen who died from a DUI last week. Unfortunately, hurt and its effects are something we cannot avoid and are products of our world. Sometimes we've been hurt intentionally, sometimes through negligence and other times our hurt is merely perceived hurt.

Either way, wounds are something we've all experienced and likewise something we'd like to conquer. Pause for a moment and truthfully answer this question before reading on: Who has hurt you the most in your life? What did they do that caused you this hurt?

My greatest wounds have come from people who have made conscious choices to verbally "destroy" me. The bible says that words have the power to dictate life and death. It also talks about the tongue being full of deadly poison (James 3:8). Destructive words are especially sensitive to me because I receive love from others best through words of affirmation/encouragement; perhaps the same is true for you. With that said, finding the truth in a world chockfull of harsh words and destructive conversations is a true challenge, as we know Satan delights in bringing pain through other people's words.

Clawing our way out of the jail cell of 'unforgiveness' through the opposite action of forgiveness frees us up to love others despite their offenses. The jail cell of unforgiveness produces rotten fruit like bitterness, resentment or even worse.

But what of the failure to forgive your neighbor? **Matthew 18** examines a harsh truth.

After an appeal to his master, a man's debt is pardoned, but when this servant continues about his business, fully forgiven, he imposes a harsh sentence on his debtor.

"But he refused. Instead, he went off and had the man thrown into prison until he could pay the debt. When the other servants saw what had happened, they were outraged and went and told their master everything that had happened.

"Then the master called the servant in. 'You wicked servant,' he said, 'I canceled all that debt of yours because you begged me to. Shouldn't you have had mercy on your fellow servant just as I had on you?' In anger his master

handed him over to the jailers to be tortured, until he should pay back all he owed.

"This is how my heavenly Father will treat each of you unless you forgive your brother or sister from your heart." (Matthew 18:30-35)

We can certainly glean a lot from this story, like the chance our Father has granted us to avoid the horrors of unforgiveness. When we are hurt by someone and choose not to forgive, we lock ourselves in a jail cell. It's called the jail cell of unforgiveness. God hands us the key to get out, but it is still our choice to unlock the cell door and receive the freedom of forgiveness, lest we justify the very same treatment for ourselves that we offered our neighbor.

Prayer: Begin a time of releasing yourself and others of sins, infractions, destructive words or any other form of unforgiveness. Receive His grace and extend it to those who have hurt you.

by **Karl Diffenderfer**
Business/Life Coach & Entrepreneur
Live With Purpose Coaching, LLC

Day 4:

Courage

"But Christ is faithful as a son over God's house. And we are his house, if we hold on to our courage and the hope of which we boast." Hebrews 3:6

Often times as we go through our journey we say to our fellows, "Stay encouraged." We send words of encouragement. We pray over those who are off to fight fires, crime or wars that they may have the courage to do God's will. In fact, one of the most powerful and simple prayers ever put to paper, commonly known as the Serenity Prayer, invokes God to grant the praying person "the serenity to accept the things I cannot change, the courage to change the things I can, and the wisdom to know the difference."

So what do we mean by courage? It's clearly an important word, as the book of Hebrews notes in the excerpt above that God lives within is – but only "if we hold on to our courage." Like many words in the English language, courage finds its origins in a word that came about by mixing two languages – in this case, Old English and French. Its root is "core" – meaning of the heart or "the seat of feelings." It's where cardiac comes from, too. In other words, when God urges us to be encouraged by His great promise, He is telling us to stay "in the heart." And as any athlete will tell you, from a golfer to a running back to a marathon runner, a strong core and heart is critical to success.

Paul echoes the writer of Hebrews when he notes in Philippians that "I eagerly expect and hope that I will be in no way ashamed, but will have sufficient courage so that now as always Christ will be exalted in my body." And what does this courage look like? Paul goes on to write in the same book that "If you have any encouragement from being united with Christ" – any, that is, any bit whatsoever, from the tiniest mustard seed on up – "then make my joy complete by being like-minded, having the same love, being one in spirit and purpose" (**Philippians 2:1-2**). If only each of us in the Church, he says, each of us different but all of whom know that Christ lives inside, can stay encouraged – can hold on to our hearts – we will "shine like stars in the universe" (**Philippians 2:15**).

That's a great promise, and one that I hope you take to heart.

Prayer: God, grant me an inside track to this wondrous promise, that courage become common to my life, and that I'm able, with the power of your Holy Spirit, to hold onto my heart.

by **Kevin Sunday**
Government Affairs Manager

Laying on of Hands   *

"Therefore let us leave the elementary doctrine of Christ and go on to maturity, not laying again a foundation of repentance from dead works and of faith toward God, and of instruction about washings, the laying on of hands, the resurrection of the dead, and eternal judgment." **(Hebrews 6:1-3)**

As the foundational Hebrews 6 text inserts, the teaching or act of Laying on of Hands was an elementary one to the Acts church and one that was not to be revisited on the journey to maturity, according to Paul. This raises my eyebrows when I try to reconcile something that's a basic tenet, in contrast to something that's rarely talked about or put into practice now. There are numerous biblical references to the act (and not merely the symbol) of the laying on of hands, with mainly three functions.

1. **Healing the sick** (Mark 16:17-18, Acts 28:8)
2. **Impartation** (1st Timothy 4:14, Acts 8:17)
3. **The "send-off" prayer** (Acts 13:3, Acts 6:6)

There is a common thread, no matter which prayer the "handlers" were going after: they all had to do with the Holy Spirit. Through the power of the Holy Spirit, Jesus, the disciples and the apostles healed the sick. Through the transfer of an active Holy Spirit at the dawn of Pentecost, new Christians were being filled or 'imparted.' Through the boldness and commission available through the Holy Spirit, saints were being sent off to preach the good news to a hostile world.

It should do much for the re-positioning or reordering of our perspective to know that this was basic to Paul's disciples. The laying on of hands was one of the things these guys and gals learned in elementary or grade school, building upon it and other principal tenets in order to reach a place of maturity in the faith. So the folks that Paul (or the author of Hebrews) is addressing in chapter 6 had graduated, or were well on their way, from the school of fundamentals and were now more concerned with manifesting the fruits and gifts of the spirit.

Striking a balance in our ministerial diets

So, what can we do about it, other than laying hands on our brothers and sisters? I think in many ways we would do well for ourselves in imitating the early church. In fact, Paul calls on his constituents to imitate him (**1st Corinthians 4:16**). So, in coming into alignment with basic teaching, we can begin to mature and yield fruit in the order with which God provided: by knowing and applying the foundation, and when we've mastered it, simply building upon it.

Prayer: Ruminate in His wisdom and expansiveness today as you go about your routine: what is it [God] that I need to know and believe in order to grow and mature in the faith? Pray that He reveals these things to you and that you'd have the faith to obey that which He uncovers.

"Even if you had ten thousand guardians in Christ, you do not have many fathers, for in Christ Jesus I became your father through the gospel. Therefore I urge you to imitate me."
1 Corinthians 4:15-16

by **Joe D'Orsie**
Communications & Spiritual Life Counsel
Live With Purpose Coaching, LLC

Spiritual Fruit

Where does good spiritual fruit come from, truly? It is pretty easy to pinpoint. It's found in children of God who live lives led by the Holy Spirit.

"Those who live by way of the Spirit will not gratify the desires of the sinful nature of man. For the sinful nature desires what is contrary to the Spirit, and the Spirit what is contrary to the sinful nature. They are in conflict with each other, so that you do not do what you want." **Galatians 5:16-17**

But if you are led by the Spirit, you are not under the law (v.18). There is true freedom for those who embrace a life empowered and led daily by the Spirit. It is counterintuitive to the stubborn will of man, our selfish ambitions, our unsatisfied craving for more earthly treasures or worldly comforts (though they are many times mere desires vs. actual needs). If we look at Scripture we begin to better understand God's character, His desire for how we should live and just what good spiritual fruit should look like.

²²But the fruit of the Spirit is love, joy, peace, patience, kindness, goodness, faithfulness, ²³gentleness and self-control. Against such things there is no law. ²⁴Those who belong to Christ Jesus have crucified the sinful nature with its passions and desires. ²⁵Since we live by the Spirit, let us keep in step with the Spirit. ²⁶Let us not become conceited, provoking and envying each other. **Galatians 5:22-26**

You don't need to struggle to live free. Dump the baggage of trying to live up to the standards of the world, and dare to completely take God at His written word. Period.

As we see in Galatians 5:23 - Against the stated fruit of the Spirit, there is no such law! Does that excite you? If that doesn't get you truly excited, then I challenge you to spend quiet time today in prayer with God asking Him to help you better understand the reality of the freedom that is available to those who abide in Christ, and accept who He was, is and what He has done for them. They understand that they received the empowerment of the Holy Spirit, who dwells richly within their temple (their body).

Walking out life in the Spirit allows you to walk forward in an amazing journey anchored in true, lasting freedom! A byproduct of that reality is the evidence of good spiritual fruit in our lives each day. We can stand out in the world and direct our lives to the evidence of the love and power of the one true God, and see the world we encounter receive that revelation through our lives!

Prayer: Father, thank you for the possibility of a bountiful harvest of fruit in my life. Fine tune me and prune me to yield any and all of your fruits, according to your purpose.

"But the fruit of the Spirit is love, joy, peace, patience, kindness, goodness, faithfulness, gentleness and self-control. Against such things there is no law."
Galatians 5:22-23

by **Joseph Sharp**
International Business/Life Coach, Speaker & Author
Live With Purpose Coaching, LLC

Watchfulness

Being watchful is a very important spiritual discipline whether you believe we are members of the "end time" church or not. Jesus noted the need for being watchful when His disciples were asking him about the future. (See Mark 13:32-37). In fact, watchfulness dominated much of Paul's writings so much so that they conveyed urgency not just in requiring action, but also doing so with haste. (See Romans 13:11-14)

Another reason for watchfulness, evident in Paul's correspondence with the early church, is the reoccurring theme of guarding against "falling away." The watchdogs of the early church, leaders and laypeople alike, were sensing the imposing falsehoods of counterfeit movements. 'Falling away' seems to be a very severe topic for the apostles, usually coupled in scripture with exhortations against false teaching. Because of its clear emphasis, it's something that we should seriously weigh. In fact, the author of Hebrews inserts that it's impossible to be restored back to the faith once we've fallen away:

"For it is impossible to restore again to repentance those

who have once been enlightened, and have tasted the goodness of the word of God and the powers of the age to come, and then have fallen away, since on their own they are crucifying again the Son of God and are holding him up to contempt." **Hebrews 6:4-6 NRSV**

Take a moment to seek God in identifying any area of your faith where you could be losing ground to the enemy. Pray that it be exposed and that a Godly watchfulness be instilled in your heart and a solid and complete faith be built anew to avoid the dangers of falling away. Keep yourself accountable in this, free from fear, but watchful of the schemes of the enemy. You can use Galatians 5:22-23 as a filter to determine whether or not you're manifesting maturity in the faith.

Are you loving, joyous, making peace, patient in mind and body, kind, exuding goodness, exhibiting faith, showing gentleness, and practicing self-control?

Prayer: Comb your mind and heart, with the help of the Holy Spirit, and identify people you may know that could be showing symptoms of falling away. You can reference 2nd Timothy 2 and 3 to help you identify some characteristics of a person that could be on the brink of falling away. Intercede on their behalf that they would return to the simple and evident truth that they knew before.

by **Joe D'Orsie**
Communications & Spiritual Life Counsel
Live With Purpose Coaching, LLC

Obedience

"Samuel said, "Has the LORD as much delight in burnt offerings and sacrifices As in obeying the voice of the LORD? Behold, to obey is better than sacrifice, And to heed than the fat of rams." **1 Samuel 15:22 NASB**

For most people, the word obedience carries a lot of negative connotation. It can imply control or dominance. It can even conjure up memories of being severely punished when an act of obedience wasn't carried out. In our relationship with God, however, it's the backbone and heartbeat of a father and son relationship.

Jesus, Our Example:

Jesus and the Father were close and within this relationship Jesus illustrated what obedience looked like. Jesus, Himself, used the following words to convey this idea:

John 5:19 – Therefore Jesus answered and was saying to them, "Truly, truly, I say to you, the Son can do nothing of Himself, unless it is something He sees the Father doing; for whatever the Father does, these things the Son also does in like manner."

John 8:28 – "When you lift up the Son of Man, then you will know that I am He, and I do nothing on My own initiative, but I speak these things as the Father taught Me."

In order for Jesus to have seen what it was that His father was doing and hear what it was that His Father was saying, He would have had to be in relationship with His Father. And as the Father was communicating with His Son, faith was present with Jesus to carry out His Father's commands.

Abiding – The Secret to a Life of Relational Obedience:

In John 15, Jesus explains the recipe for what a lifestyle of relational obedience looks like. He uses the analogy of a vine and branches to illustrate that obedience and fruit-bearing are only accomplished if we stay connected to Him and abide in His love (see John 15:1-5). As a result, the Father is glorified when we bear much fruit and it is also the evidence that we are Jesus' disciples (see John 15:8). When we are obedient to what the Father asks us to do out of a relationship with Him, the reward is twofold (see John 15:10-11):

1. We will abide in His love because our conscience is clean.
2. We will have joy and it will be made full.

Indeed, obedience is the evidence that we are abiding in the love of God and likewise applying our love for Him. It's the byproduct of relationship. Jesus says this in John 14:21, "He who has my commandments and keeps them is the one who loves Me; and he who loves Me will be loved by My Father, and I will love him and will disclose Myself to him." If obedience causes Jesus to reveal Himself to me in a greater way, sign me up!

To consider in **prayer:**

1. Everything Jesus did and said was shown to Him and said to Him out of His relationship with His father.
2. Jesus' mission on the earth was to be obedient to the One who sent Him and to fulfill why He was sent.
3. Obedience requires humility and the surrender of your will.
4. You were created to hear and to be in fellowship with your Father and obey out of a mutual, loving relationship.
5. Intimacy with God is the key to relational obedience and the bearing of fruit.

by **Brian Connolly**
Pastor & Author

Day 9:

Faith - The faith/works harmony

See James 2: 14-26

James chapter two more than adequately addresses the paradox of faith and works, which, when you think about it, really isn't even a paradox. It only has existed as one in the history of the church because we have allowed it to. The reason this point of dissension is so unfortunate is because these two should coexist in perfect harmony rather than stand as two converse principles. Faith and works are interdependent on each other. Note James' repeated points in James 2:14-26 (NRSV)

- Faith by itself, without works, is dead (17)
- Faith apart from works is barren (20)
- Abraham was justified by the works made manifest by his faith (21)
- Abraham's faith was brought to completion by works (22)
- A person is justified by works and not by faith alone (24)
- Faith without works is dead (26)

In the words of my pastor, "you manifest what you believe." What a convicting thought! If my actions, or works, do not match my words and inner motives, then I risk nullifying them. Abraham, the father of our faith, was actually prepared to sacrifice his son Isaac, he didn't just talk about it and proclaim it. The grittiness of faith becomes evident when we practice it. Be prepared to risk, sacrifice, and above all, love.

Jesus said: "If you love me, you will keep my commandments." (see John 14:15) Keeping His commandments requires action, not just words.

Prayer: Think about an area of your faith where your words may precede your actions. Ask for forgiveness in this area of malpractice, and pray for faith to exercise what you believe.

by **Joe D'Orsie**
Communications & Spiritual Life Counsel
Live With Purpose Coaching, LLC

Suffering

"In this you greatly rejoice, even though now for a little while, if necessary, you have been distressed by various trials, that the proof of your faith, being more precious than gold which is perishable, even though tested by fire, may be found to result in praise and glory and honor at the revelation of Jesus Christ." ***1 Peter 1:6-7***

How can suffering turn into joy?

In many countries, 24 karat gold is the standard or measuring stick for making jewelry, due to its color and quality. In others however, 14 karat is preferred due to its hardness and strength since unalloyed gold bends more easily. So why does God want us purer and cleaner?

When our faith is tested it should produce patience and endurance, but for some people testing, trials and tribulation produce bitterness, unforgiveness, resentment and discouragement. Attitudes become rigid and inflexible, turning hearts tough, impenetrable and obstinate. Our faith, just like gold, gets overpowered and adulterated by other elements that hinder its flexibility and capacity to reach immeasurable heights.

Suffering does not cause joy, but if we learn to see suffering as the process God uses to help us be more bendable to His will and less resistant to love, forgiveness and trust, in due time we will reap a harvest of joy as we reach maturity and share in Jesus' glory.

- Suffering 'examines' our faith, which turns into steadfastness (James 1: 2-4)
- Suffering yields endurance, builds character and increases hope (Romans 5:3-5)
- Suffering reminds us of Christ's suffering (1 Peter 4:13)
- Suffering increases our dependability and trust in God (2 Corinthians 12:10)
- Suffering for Christ strengthens our connection with God and His Spirit (1 Peter 4:14)

As you consider or remember the sorrows and distress you have experienced in your life reflect on how they have shaped you. Did they change you in a positive or negative way? Are they still affecting you? Have they made you less sensitive to others' needs and pain? Do you harbor rancor in your heart due to a past hurt? Have you allowed rebellion or a sense of entitlement toward God to come into your heart? Or perhaps, you are holding our Heavenly Father responsible for past wrongs and your relationship with Him has grown distant and cold?

Prayer: Take a moment and undergo 'spiritual inventory.' Ask the Lord to search your heart, for He is always ready and willing. Don't be afraid to ask specific things and hear specific answers!

"In this you greatly rejoice, even though now for a little while, if necessary, you have been distressed by various trials."
1 Peter 1:6-7

by **Gina Paredes**
Coaching Support & Prayer Specialist
Live With Purpose Coaching, LLC

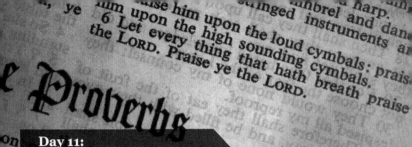

Wisdom

I recently read the underside of a bottle cap which quoted a famous physician. The statement read: "Knowledge is the process of piling up facts; wisdom lies in their simplification." I don't believe that this statement is wholly untrue, as I do believe that many biblical truths are very simple and faith many times rests in the simplicity of the Gospel. Over-analysis and over thinking can tend to fog the integrity of the truth to the person that's exercising their mind over their heart. However, Job 28:28 answers our question about wisdom here directly:

*"...**the fear of the Lord, that is wisdom**; and to depart from evil is understanding." **Job 28:28**

Let me paraphrase: reverence, esteem and obedience to our Heavenly Father IS wisdom, and repentance and holiness is understanding.

I can agree in part with the bottle cap quote; there is simplicity in the knowledge of the truth because truth is a person: the person of Jesus. So wisdom is found in obeying His commands and revering his sovereignty and authority. Remember: The disciples' final instructions were not to teach others the Lord's commandments– they were to teach them to obey the Lord's commandments. (Matthew 28:29) So wisdom, in essence, is simply obedience, because to fear the Lord one must desire to abide in Him and make Him proud, which only comes by faith made real through everyday obedience. The fear of the Lord has to do with awe, not anxiety, so be careful not to cloud the fear of the lord with something that brings condemnation. Besides, God is love, and love is the nemesis of fear. (1st John 4).

Prayer: Take a moment to reflect on how the world defines wisdom and how the Word of God defines wisdom. Are there any areas in your life where you need to allow your heart to take precedent over your head? Pray for humility in this and for God to guide you in true wisdom, so that you would stand in awe and revere Him daily.

by **Joe D'Orsie**
Communications & Spiritual Life Counsel
Live With Purpose Coaching, LLC

Holiness

Colossians 1:22

"Yet now he has reconciled you to himself through the death of Christ in his physical body. As a result, he has brought you into his own presence, and you are holy and blameless as you stand before him without a single fault."

"You are HOLY and BLAMELESS as you stand before Him without a SINGLE FAULT." Those are some weighty words! The Word of God is full of reminders that we indeed are holy because of our reconciliation to God through Christ, and yet many believers are hesitant to call themselves so.

Whether we feel comfortable calling ourselves holy or not, the fact is that our Father knew, loved, and chose us long ago, and His Spirit has made us holy (1 Peter 1:2). It's a done deal. Once we understand the truth of those words, our striving to become holy ceases and we more naturally begin to demonstrate holiness in our lives.

Indeed, we are evermore becoming like Jesus, therefore, becoming more and more holy. But what if that transformation happens less because of <u>what we DO</u>, and more because of the understanding of <u>who we ARE</u>? What if we walk out holiness in a more natural way once we realize and believe that it is part of our new nature? The pressure to "be holy, as I am holy" no longer seems like an unattainable goal, but rather an invitation from the Lord to glorify Himself, as He reminds us of our true identity in Him.

Prayer: Lord, I thank you for who you have already made me in you. I thank you that I am holy, and will only become more holy as I believe and meditate on the truth that I stand in front of you without a single fault.

by **Adrienne D'Orsie**
HOPE International

Day 13:

Communication

Many sections of scripture speak to how we are to communicate as believers. The very lifeblood of our ministry is to convey truth through words. Our Lord Jesus is the Word of God, existent even at the dawning of time. Being created in His image gives us the access and permission to wield the sword of truth and season our words and conversations with grace *and* truth. Here are a few characteristics of how we are to communicate to those around us and some things to be watchful of in our daily communicative interactions:

1. **Letting your Yes be Yes, and your No, No** (Matt.5:37) – Saying what you mean and meaning what you say.

   Red Flags: excessive sarcasm, half-truths, making empty promises, etc.

2. **Bridling your tongue** (James Chapter 1) – Listening primarily and not being quick and over-zealous to retort and/or argue, etc.

Red Flags: being prone to quarrelling, making statements that you regret later, the presence of anger, bitterness and resentment in your words and effectively your life.

3. **Applying the Golden Rule to your conversations** – Communicating with the express intent of edifying your neighbor.

   Red Flags: one-dimensional conversations, conversations not aligned with selflessness, conversations where you're talking much more than you are listening, etc.

4. **'Death and Life are in the power of the tongue; and they that love it shall eat its fruit'** (Proverbs 18:21) - Dictating your path and speaking life rather than death.

   Red Flags: sowing death with your words, being habitually pessimistic, submitting to a victim's mentality in word and deed, etc.

Think about your daily interactions and conversations. Are there any red flags listed above that you are guilty of? It's easy to slip into these craftily conceived snares which tend to bring about destruction and division relationally, but we're capable of Christ-like communication.

*Create a list of areas where you could improve in your communication and compare them with some of the ways you communicate (i.e in person, phone, E-mail). What practical ways can you improve and what areas should you pray for heart transformation in? Record your findings and be accountable to holding your conversations up to the template set forth by the one true conversationalist. Jesus.

Prayer: God, manifest yourself through the words that flow through my mouth and give me new understanding about honoring and representing you with my tongue.

"All you need to say is simply 'Yes' or 'No'; anything beyond this comes from the evil one."
Matthew 5:37

by **Joe D'Orsie**
Communications & Spiritual Life Counsel
Live With Purpose Coaching, LLC

Resurrection of the Dead   *

Jesus coined the phrase and set the stage

Jesus and His ascension from the grave to take His position at the Father's right hand is a major tenet not just of our creeds and hymns, but of our faith. It was through this act that the grave was overcome, the Holy Spirit was unleashed, the power of the enemy was dissolved and long anticipated prophecies were confirmed.

Resurrection is so important to the Gospel that Paul says these things in **1st Corinthians 15**:

"…if Christ has not been raised, our preaching is useless and so is your faith." **(15:14)**

"…if Christ has not been raised, your faith is futile; you are still in your sins." **(15:17)**

Jesus' resurrection is a big deal. He didn't remain powerless, hanging on a cross, subject to His persecutors. He rose, the veil was torn and His repeated foretelling of His death and resurrection proved true. He conquered the grave and the very same spirit that accomplished His ascent came to earth on the day of Pentecost and was received by the fledgling Christian Church.

"And if the Spirit of him who raised Jesus from the dead is living in you, he who raised Christ from the dead will also give life to your mortal bodies because of his Spirit who lives in you." **Romans 8:11**

Why is death important?

To paraphrase Paul: Where's your sting death?

Because 'death' doesn't have the final say means that we can rest assuredly in the hope of eternal life, laid out masterfully by King Jesus. And, because He preceded us in this He has come to take first place in the glory of eternity, as an example for us to follow in the fullness of time.

So if death isn't the prevailing topic of our life legacy, why and how could it ever be a cause for worry?

"The sun has one kind of splendor, the moon another and the stars another; and star differs from star in splendor.

So will it be with the resurrection of the dead. The body that is sown is perishable, it is raised imperishable; it is sown in dishonor, it is raised in glory; it is sown in weakness, it is raised in power; it is sown a natural body, it is raised a spiritual body." **1st Corinthians 15:41-44**

We have a lot to look forward to! We'll be resurrected in a manner that's imperishable, glorious and powerful! Death and its teachings pale in comparison to the guarantee of eternal life, and that should be the lens with which we see things daily.

Prayer: Father, give me your perspective today; one that sees and filters the world through abundant life and things eternal. Show me how to not hold mere death in high regard.

by **Joe D'Orsie**
Communications & Spiritual Life Counsel
Live With Purpose Coaching, LLC

Endurance

The writer of Hebrews sums it up pretty well in chapter 12, verses 1 & 2 (ESV) "Therefore, since we are surrounded by so great a cloud of witnesses, let us also lay aside every weight and sin which clings so closely, and let us **run with endurance** the race that is set before us, looking to Jesus, the founder and perfecter of our faith, who for the joy that was set before him endured the cross, despising the shame, and is seated at the right hand of the throne of God."

Read **Hebrews 2:3-17** for an even greater challenge.

Whenever the topic of **Endurance** is brought up one can't help but run to the life of Paul the Apostle. Beaten, stoned, shipwrecked, adrift at sea, imprisoned. You name it. It all started with a visit from God and an affliction of blindness. Ah, but what a result. An epic picture of transformation and renewal: the greatest persecutor of Christians to the greatest apostle and evangelist of that time, maybe of all time. There's so much to be gleaned from Paul's life and his willingness to stand firm in the faith.

I had an opportunity recently to visit India. I was struck by the contrast between our way of life in the United States and the "accepted" way of life among the people in the remote villages around Bangalore. I would characterize it as abject poverty. Sleeping under tarps on the dirt, scraping to make it day to day. That's endurance. We complain here if we get caught in traffic for an extra 15 minutes at rush hour.

There are outcomes in life that we reap from sowing bad seeds and there are those that happen just because there's sin in this world. We are called to endure in every circumstance, even from the spiritual warfare that comes our way out of obedience to God. That's what Paul endured.

Let's lift up our eyes and thank God for all that comes our way. We were never promised a trouble-free life as believers in Jesus Christ but we ARE promised a life of fulfillment, love and abundance far beyond material things.

Prayer: Thank God that He's the wind under our wings and the strength in our life to endure all things through Christ our Savior. Ask Him to be present when you endure trials, tribulations and challenges, so that He is even glorified in your weakness or vulnerability.

by **Steve Adams**
Business/Life Coach & Entrepreneur
Live With Purpose Coaching, LLC

Identity

Sound identity is a must-have precursor to spiritual fruit and an effective relationship with God and others. It's much easier to step into your destiny and yield good fruit when you know who you are and why. One of my spiritual fathers once said, speaking of a tree and its fruit, "God doesn't make bad trees." If we're living in this identity reality, that we are good trees created to produce good fruit, we've overcome one of Satan's go-to lies: that our identity isn't rooted in Christ. Likewise, a lack of sound identity is the root of many hindrances in your relationships and ministry, and can naturally fog your perception from the inside out.

*"Love the Lord your God with all your heart and with all your soul and with all your mind. This is the first and greatest commandment. And the second is like it: 'Love your neighbor as yourself. All the Law and the Prophets hang on these two commandments." **Matthew 22:37-40***

The Greatest Commandment - paraphrased

1. Love God with all that you have (heart, soul & mind)
2. Love your neighbor as yourself

With all notions of false humility aside, consider the heart of the second "greatest" commandment. Love your neighbor as yourself. Is this commandment not dependent on you first loving and valuing yourself? Your place in the body of Christ. Your spiritual gifts. Your ministry. Your purpose. Your destiny. Don't confuse this with an over-individualistic "me" mentality; this is simply taking God at His word. You have permission to love yourself, because He first loved you: all of the law and the prophets depend on it!

"We love because he first loved us." **1 John 4:19**

Think of it this way: In order to be obedient in loving your neighbor, you must first meet the criteria of loving yourself; the command is a conditional one. In fact, we know that to best love our neighbor, according to the 'red letters' in Matthew 22, mirroring how we love ourselves is a good start.

Prayer: If you haven't before, ask God who you are. How are you set apart? What is your function in the body of Christ? How has He wired you and what hereditary traits do you have that were passed down by your Father in Heaven? What has He created you to do?

by **Joe D'Orsie**
Communications & Spiritual Life Counsel
Live With Purpose Coaching, LLC

The Power of a Clear Conscience

"¹³Whoever conceals their sins does not prosper, but the one who confesses and renounces them finds mercy."
Proverbs 28:13

Proverbs 28:13 keeps it pretty simple for readers. Mercy and grace is found through confession and true repentance.

"Whatever your sin is or whatever lie you are entertaining, God wants to take it from you. In fact, He already bore every mistake we've ever made or will make on the cross. Our role is to simply bring it before him with an attitude of repentance." **Psalm 32:5**

How destructive is a darkened conscience? In Genesis we see the very first example of sin and the need for repentance. Adam and Eve recognized they were in sin and ran and hid themselves from God. They were covered with shame immediately.

"Sin that we have failed to confess to God will only keep us separated from God." Isaiah 59:2

Why do we hold so tightly to something so deadly? Satan is a great deceiver. His main tactic is to divide or separate us from our lifeline, God, who makes us effective in carrying out His will and functioning as His body. Separation from God causes identity problems.

We remain in the bondage of sin and we begin to lose our identity in Christ. (Proverbs 23:7) This is one of Satan's greatest victories when he convinces a child of God that they are no longer worthy of the Father's love.

We can't be a great light to the world and become all that God has called us to be if we are weighted down by unresolved sin. Have you ever tried to witness or take a stand for God while tightly clutching to a behavior God is asking you to lay down at His feet? The word hypocrite comes to mind often, accompanied by a sick feeling in your stomach. **Sin, in which we have not repented from, robs our testimony in Christ. (1 Peter 3:15-16)**

Think of a foggy conscience as a one lane road clogged with debris and a clear conscience as an unobstructed four lane highway. A driver has greater access to his/her destination in the latter route. Likewise, we tend to be, and rightly so, more able and available to approach God and act in accordance with Him when we've been cleared of any sin, guilt, condemnation, etc.

In effect, with a clear conscience we can stand

confident before God and man. (1 John 3:20-22)

A Clear Conscience will:

1. Strengthen our Spirit
2. Enhance our leadership and influence in the church
3. Cause our lives and work to prosper
4. Cause our words to edify others
5. Enable us to operate in wisdom
6. Enable us to touch the lives of those we know and encounter

   (See Proverbs 10)

Prayer: Take some time to search your heart. Ask God to reveal any sin in your life you need to place before His feet. Make a commitment today to take the steps toward leading a blameless life. Acts 24:16 – So I strive always to keep my conscience clear before God and man.

by **Charity Fox**
Coaching Support & Prayer Specialist
Live With Purpose Coaching, LLC

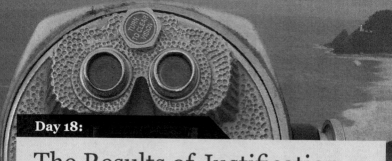

The Results of Justification

In Romans 5, we see the famous declaration that we have been made righteous in the sight of God **by (5:9)** the blood of Jesus and **through (5:1)** faith. An elementary yet often misunderstood truth is found simply in the tense of verbs in this passage. Through the act of Jesus' death and resurrection (5:9) and our belief in that act (5:1), we NOW can lay claim to these blessings and are thus made right in His sight. This is true once and for all for those who believe. These results of justification are present truths, not history lessons or longings of what is to come (although they do embody both history and prophecy).

Since now, having been justified... (5:9)

- We have peace with God (5:1)
- We have gained access by faith into this Grace (5:2)
- We boast in hope of the Glory of God (5:2)
- We glory in our sufferings (5:3)
- We possess a Hope that doesn't put us to shame (5:5)
- We have God's Love pouring into our hearts (5:5)
- We are saved from God's wrath (5:9)
- We are reconciled to him (5:10-11)

At face value, these things are unparalleled truths; they are present realities for those who believe that they are present realities. And, if you, in the moment, say yes to the results paid for on the cross, you cannot at the same time be hopeless, unbelieving, condemned and separated from God.

Understanding Justification

Some common American church phraseologies that can be chalked up as basic misunderstandings are phrases like "that's just human nature," and "we're all sinners." Not only do these phrases give us permission to act like the world and to perpetuate a sinful lifestyle, but they object to what 'justification' actually is, as described by this passage and many others. Sin and humanness are no longer natural things to the believer who hears and does the things that are revealed to them in passages like Romans 5. Why? Because we've been justified, and we've been justified because Jesus said so and did so.

Prayer: Choose to be justified today. Ask God about your journey of justification and pray that He reveal to you the things that you are and the things that you aren't. Receive justification just as you would forgiveness and prepare to act on it today.

by **Joe D'Orsie**
Communications & Spiritual Life Counsel
Live With Purpose Coaching, LLC

Day 19:

Righteousness

In Exchange for Independence

"Now I take limitations in stride, and with good cheer, these limitations that cut me down to size - abuse, accidents, opposition, bad breaks. I just let Christ take over! And so the weaker I get, the stronger I become." ***2 Corinthians 12:10 MSG***

In my early walk with Christ my weaknesses and limitations would cause me to go wayward. I desired to be like other Christians who were disciplined in fasting, fervent in prayer and consistent in attending church. But whenever I failed to meet these expectations I set for myself, I would get frustrated and stop looking for God. I was convinced that God was wasting His time on a walking mess who showed no improvement. But one day God revealed to me how grace through Jesus' victory on the cross really works. To say the least, it changed my Christian walk forever. I stopped relying on works and began to understand that nothing can make me holier, cleaner and more righteous than relying on God.

'Matryoshkas' Russian Dolls are wooden figures which separate, top from bottom, to reveal a smaller figure of the same sort nestled inside. In the same way, when we accept Jesus He comes and coats us with His righteousness, enabling us to shed our humanity and take on His image. It's this conforming to His will that allows us to become a better version of ourselves as we grow in Him and step into His full stature. His love, strength, power and authority become instantly available in exchange for our complete trust and dependence on Him. Believing, seeking, relying, pursuing and choosing Jesus every day is what makes us righteous.

Here are some other characteristics of attaining righteousness:

- Believing what the Lord tells us, counts as righteousness. **Genesis 15:6-10**.
- Seeking the Lord is pursuing righteousness. **Isaiah 51:1**
- Knowing His righteousness identifies us as one with Him, sharing in His righteousness. **1 John 2:29**
- Depending on Christ turns us into the righteousness of God. **2 Cor. 5:21**
- Remaining in Christ revives our spirit because of righteousness. **Romans 8:10**

It's an unfair (and easy) exchange to surrender our autonomy for all God has to offer, yet thousands of people struggle to do so all their lives. Where do you find yourself today, fighting for independence or victorious in righteousness? Let Jesus take over and trade your burdens for His yoke. This is the only way you will find rest and righteousness.

Prayer: Lord, lead me down the path of righteousness. Make it apparent to me today how to put on righteousness and see its effects.

"But if Christ is in you, then even though your body is subject to death because of sin, the Spirit gives life because of righteousness."
Romans 8:10

by **Gina Paredes**
Coaching Support & Prayer Specialist
Live With Purpose Coaching, LLC

Day 20:

Forgiveness - Part II

God commands us to forgive each other over and over again (seventy times seven). Unfortunately, there are many believers who say they have forgiven someone but still find their hearts ensnared with resentment toward their offender. I would like to say that that is NOT forgiveness. If you cannot desire for God to bless that person MORE than yourself, then you are not walking in forgiveness. If your words and actions toward them do not reflect love and impartiality, then you probably haven't forgiven them.

The most devastating part of unforgiveness is that it actually hurts us more than it hurts the other party. The offender usually has already moved on from the event (or many times they're ignorant of it) while we're the ones left in the pits. That is exactly what Satan wants. Unforgiveness is like drinking poison with the intention of poisoning the other person; it's deception at its best, or worst, depending on how you look at it. Most importantly, unforgiveness keeps us from a close relationship with others as well as Papa God.

Here are the levels of unforgiveness that we can see in scripture.

Different types of unforgiveness

- The first level is unforgiveness. This is where we downright choose not to forgive. (Proverbs 24:17)

- The second level is judgement. Maybe it is a statement like "No man can be trusted" or "My sister always has to have things her way." Sometimes we pass judgment on God by saying things like "If God cared He would..." (Matthew 7:1-5)

- The third level is revenge. Maybe we give the silent treatment to our spouse or purposefully cut someone off on the highway. (references - Romans 12:19, Hebrews 10:30)

- The fourth level is inner vows. This is when we say things like "I'm never going to...." (reference - Leviticus 5:4-6)

- The fifth level is when we choose to dishonor our parents, our spouse or an authority figure. (reference - Ephesians 5:33, Romans 13:1-7)

- The sixth level is dishonoring God (reference - Romans 2:23, Psalm 51:4)

When we choose not to forgive we remain stagnant in a position of captivity and invite things like judgment, revenge and dishonor. We're able to trade these reactions, which may even seem natural sometimes, for the perfect example of forgiveness, selflessness and humility: Jesus bearing the weight of all past and future sin on the cross. This is an awesome and very much available substitute for living in bondage to unforgiveness!

So how do we forgive?

1 John 1:9 – Confess your sins of unforgiveness to the father - We need to verbalize our unforgiveness by saying "Forgive me Father for harboring unforgiveness. I choose to forgive this person for their actions toward me."

James 5:16 – "Confess your sins to each other and pray for each other's hearts that you may be healed" – Ask the person you've held unforgiveness toward to forgive you and ask if you can pray for their heart to be healed from your sin against them. In certain situations, this may be impossible to do in person, so a simple prayer of blessing and healing spoken aloud for that person would be appropriate.

Above all, we need to Love people. Loving them includes keeping no record of wrongs. Living in a way that's selfless actually involves a degree of selflessness! Go forth today and forgive freely!

Prayer: Lord, bring to my mind those that I must forgive and thus free from the bondage of unforgiveness. Forgive me for losing sight of my holy charge to not hold people's words or actions against them.

by **Karl Diffenderfer**
Business/Life Coach & Entrepreneur
Live With Purpose Coaching, LLC

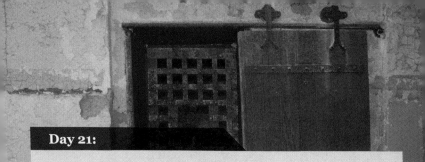

Eternal Judgment   *

Whether it's comfortable or not, hell is a dominant theme in the gospels. It's also one of the leading reasons why people are driven away from the church; it's a topic equated with 'fire and brimstone,' and other "Churchy," taboo terms and phrases that are way too often passed off as legalist. It's also rarely preached or taught about and the most popular books (that I have knowledge of) about it seem to want to explain it away or assuage it. Imagine a New York Times Bestseller about chaff being separated from wheat and burnt to a crisp by an unquenchable and never-ending fire. Non-believers don't want to hear it and believers don't want to talk about it, but it is so very real.

A 'Hell' word study in scripture reveals a few terms that are overwhelmingly recurrent: eternal, fire, death, destruction, & weeping and gnashing of teeth, to name a few. To acknowledge hell as being real and more than just marginally unsatisfactory is biblical, no matter how many Universalist commentaries you read!

- **2nd Thessalonians 1:9** – Eternal destruction and

separation
- **Matthew 10:28** – Destruction of both the soul and the body
- **Matthew 13:42/13:50** – A blazing furnace with weeping and gnashing of teeth
- **Matthew 25:41** – Eternal fire
- **Jude 1:7** – Suffering a punishment of eternal fire
- **Revelation 21:8** – Death from a fiery lake

How about a sense of urgency?

Paul consistently appeals to the early congregations with urgency and even anxiety because they knew the time and the season; that they were closer to judgment day than ever before. (Romans 13:11) Shouldn't the idea of eternal judgment provoke a similar sense of urgency in us as it did Paul and the early church? Do we realize what's at stake, that on that day when we all have to give an account for our lives, a sea of people will meet a horrifying interminable fate?

In Matthew 25 Jesus describes the moment of judgment which will determine eternity:

"Then he will say to those on his left, 'Depart from me, you who are cursed, into the eternal fire prepared for the devil and his angels. For I was hungry and you gave me nothing to eat, I was thirsty and you gave me nothing to drink, I was a stranger and you did not invite me in, I needed clothes and you did not clothe me, I was sick and in prison and you did not look after me.'

"They also will answer, 'Lord, when did we see you hungry or thirsty or a stranger or needing clothes or sick or in prison, and did not help you?'

"He will reply, 'Truly I tell you, whatever you did not do for one of the least of these, you did not do for me.'

"Then they will go away to eternal punishment, but the righteous to eternal life." **Matthew 25:41-46**

The reality evident in this gospel parable should draw us to do two things in how we conduct ourselves in our remaining days:

1. Take the position of righteousness through salvation – so that we have eternal life
2. Entreat the unrighteous – with the hope of snatching them out of the imminent and eternal fire

Prayer: God, I pray for a conviction and a certain reality to sink into the way I live my life and minister to others. God, save the lost, be patient in their shortcomings and rebellion and guide me in the way to best represent you to the lost and destitute.

by **Joe D'Orsie**
Communications & Spiritual Life Counsel
Live With Purpose Coaching, LLC

Intentionality

*"And He summoned the multitude with His disciples, and said to them, "If anyone wishes to come after Me, let him deny himself, and take up his cross, and follow Me." **Mark 8:34 NAS***

Do you think it's possible to casually lose your life for Christ every day? Saying yes to the above command by accident, leaving it up to chance or how you feel? The world will cheer us on as we pick up our cross. The flesh will join in and undergird our spirit for support. The Devil will cut us some slack as he sits back and admires our willingness to die to self. The false prophets and false teachers will take a day off in celebration of how much we accomplished. The "lust of the eyes" and the "lust of the flesh" will cut us some slack for being so diligent. Do you believe that the spirit of the anti-Christ has gone pro-Christ and that the boastful pride of life will skip to the beat all the way home? Of course not! I know that sounds like a lot but I can assure you there are no days off for the things that are set against you. These things are strategic and are waiting for an opportune time to bend your will with your thought life and emotions.

So here is my question, how intentional are you to deny yourself, pick up your cross and follow Him daily? I can guarantee you that this is not just going to casually happen. In fact, the opposite casually happens for millions of Christians every day. It could be of benefit to do a word study in the New Testament on these three phrases: be diligent, be careful, "watch out." Don't get me wrong, I don't live my life in fear of falling away but I do have awareness that whatever I am diligent toward, that is what I grow closer to. I believe it's possible to score victory over the devil in our lives and there are areas in my life where I've gained ground in enemy territory, but until I fully look like Christ, what am I waiting for?

Leonard Ravenhill, talking about discipline in prayer once said, "If the boys up at West Point can do it, can't we?" He was referring to their intentional discipline. This reminded me that I have been given a spirit of discipline, but if I am not intentional to pray, pursue, give and evangelize, then trust me, I am not just going to all of a sudden find myself doing it. The will of God is done by many but those who He strengthens are only those whose hearts are fully devoted to Him. Do you know how much intentionality it takes to fully devote your heart to Him?

Prayer: God, clear the way (distractions, idols, addictions, etc.) for me to come into a position of full devotion to you. Gear me up and prepare me, Father, for an intentional life expended to make you known on earth.

by **Adam Bower**
*Sr. Pastor of Praise Community Church, York, PA
& creator of KAIO small groups*

Day 23:

Boldness

Read Acts 4:23-31

Immediately after being "released," the believers in Acts Chapter 4 specifically prayed for boldness. So what is boldness, aside from the dictionary definition? The context in verse 29 gives us a clue. "And now, Lord, look at their threats, and grant to your servants (or slaves) to speak your word with all boldness..." **Acts 4:29 NRSV**. "They" who were applying pressure through threats to the believers were Herod and Pontius Pilate, with the Gentiles and the peoples of Israel (4:27). The antagonists of the newfound Gospel movement were causing the believers to seek boldness to speak His word. The certain and real threat of pressure had just been personified through Jesus' crucifixion and this body of new believers sought out the spiritual power to release the Kingdom on earth in the midst of constant and life-threatening force. They had just witnessed Peter and John boldly orate to an unbelieving council that they would not heed their threats to cease preaching, and they were seeking the very same Spirit of boldness in an urgent petition.

2,000 years removed from the foundation of boldness established by the great masons of our faith in Acts and elsewhere, there is still a glistening opportunity to seek boldness and act on it. Living 'contrary to popular belief' is a form of boldness in our society and a challenge to remain unshaken by the growing territory allotted to "culture." Worldliness and relativism, unfortunately, have become cultural mainstays in America and they seek to claim their rite over unchanging biblical truth. A predominant focus on doctrines like psychology, pharmaceutics, humanist ideals and "interfaith prayer" has, whether in word or deed, crowded the American believer. Here is a call for the perseverance and endurance of the saints. (See Revelation 14:12)

*"Do you not know that friendship with the world is enmity with God." **James 4:4 NRSV***

Intercede: Despite the shifts and tremors in American culture that increasingly test the American church, we still enjoy an elevated level of freedom compared with other regions of the world. There are parts of the world where a starkly similar climate exists (with that of the Acts church) where pressured and threatened Christians could use the intercession of the saints. Pause to intercede for believers in the Middle East, China and other sections of the world who face threats to their beliefs every day.

by **Joe D'Orsie**

Communications & Spiritual Life Counsel
Live With Purpose Coaching, LLC

Godliness (Being an image bearer)

God saw all that he had made, and it was very good. Genesis 1:31a

At the culmination of the creation story, God creates man and woman. And then, instead of rushing to His next task, He savors what He's done. He appraises the work of His hands, much like a workman would "survey" his creation. [1]

And what does He think of His workmanship? In response to the man and the woman, He gasps with delight. Genesis 1:31 says, God surveyed all He had made, and "it was very good."

More literally it is translated: "lo! Good very!"

It was as if God, in His pleasure, couldn't contain Himself in His revelry: "It is not merely a benediction which He utters, but an expression of admiration."[2]

Until then, Scripture had said He had considered creation "good." But when man and woman were created—the people who bear His image—He takes pleasure in them.

What? God admires us?

It's hard for me to recognize His delight in who I am. I am so prone to believe God is displeased with me, rather than recognizing He sees me as something He has created from His own hands, from the dust of the earth, from the recesses of His heart.

When he looks at you and I He shouts, "Lo! Good very" - I am pleased with you. I rejoice over you. And I delight in you.

Recently, I've been asking Him to share with me what He thinks of me. Because I cannot love, give, or serve unless I am safely rooted in His love.

And what is His response? He gasps in admiration.

He finds you and me worthy to shout over, to stop and admire, and to gasp in awe of.

In Zephaniah 3:17 it says, "The LORD your God is in your midst, A victorious warrior. He will exult over you with joy, He will be quiet in His love, He will rejoice over you with shouts of joy."

We give God joy by being who we are. I still can't understand this. But I take delight in Him as He rejoices over me.

Prayer: Lord, show me how you feel about me. I often feel unworthy in your presence, but please reveal your truth to me—the truth that you take delight in me. I thank you for making me in your image—that I am the creation you had in mind since the beginning of time. You are holy, and I give you honor and praise.

"God saw all that he had made, and it was very good."
Genesis 1:31a

by **Anna Haggard**
Destroyer of Strongholds

The Spiritual Person

*"Those who live according to the flesh have their minds set on what the flesh desires; but those who live in accordance with the Spirit have their minds set on what the Spirit desires." **Romans 8:5***

Romans 6-8 delivers a convicting contrast between the fleshly person and the spiritual person. Being completely separate, even in their nature, they cannot coexist because they are of differing kingdoms. Romans 8:5 teaches that the spiritual person, as opposed to the fleshly person, has 'their mind set on what the Spirit desires.'

Understanding that the new nature provided by rebirth in the Spirit, one could ask the viable question: does the Spirit ever desire impatience, selfishness, stress, or lust, to name a few? The answer is no, and the hope is that neither do you, as long as you are in agreement with the Spirit. The profoundness of this verse does not just imply, but states that YOU, when in accordance with the Spirit, have your mind set on what the Spirit desires. This means, as Paul describes in further detail, that your very nature changes when you are walking and living in the Spirit; you no longer take on the flesh or operate the way the flesh does because you're living in a way

The Balanced Spiritual Diet: a 30-Day Challenge   69

that's free, encouraged, joyous, and very much spiritual! So contrary to conventional wisdom, it's possible to cancel the flesh and operate solely in the Spirit, so says the Holy Bible. It's literally the blue print of Paul's letter to the Romans. This isn't optimism to the extreme, it's actually a truth that can be accessed, potentially all the time!

The characteristics of the person take on the characteristics of the Spirit in the person... In scripture the Holy Spirit testifies about these things:

- Testifies with our Spirit that we are God's children (Romans 8:16)
- I will put my laws in their hearts and write them in their minds (Hebrews 10:16)
- Their sins and lawless acts I will remember no more - and where these have been forgiven, there is no longer any sacrifice for sin (Hebrews 10:17)
- He will guide us into all truth (John 16:13)
- He will tell us what is yet to come (John 16:13)

Prayer: Take a moment to think about operating in the Spirit today. This isn't a pitch for "positive thinking," this is a pitch for your destiny through Jesus. Consider a day free of the flesh. What does it look like? What must you do to make it happen? Pray for ears to hear God's Spirit today in every situation and to think and act on what the Holy Spirit is saying, not your flesh.

by **Joe D'Orsie**
Communications & Spiritual Life Counsel
Live With Purpose Coaching, LLC

Perseverance

When thinking about true perseverance and how one commits to running the race, four questions come to mind.

1. What are you owed?
2. What do you own?
3. What do you need?
4. What have you been given?

Take any situation and put it up against these four questions and you will truly see how little life's problems are compared to the truths of God.

1. What are you owed?

Romans 3:23-24 *[23] for all have sinned and fall short of the glory of God, [24] being justified as a gift by His grace through the redemption which is in Christ Jesus...*

Does God owe you something? He created you, gives you food, protects you, supplies oxygen and the sun, not to mention gravity and everything spinning in perfect harmony. Are we entitled children, although it's His desire to give us these things? Are we owed a perfect spouse, although it's His desire to perfect us in Him. Are we owed provision, although it's His desire to provide? Are we owed answered prayers, although it's His desire to move when we petition Him? The only thing you are owed biblically is death, for penalty of your sins, and the incredible thing is that He has already paid the tab by dying on your behalf! Is He an awesome God? Absolutely!

2. What do you own?

Acts 7:49a *'Heaven is My throne, And earth is the footstool of My feet...*

The heavens are His throne and the earth is His footstool and He owns everything in it, even your own body. God has given the earth to man to steward for a time, and everything in your life: relationships, choices, money, etc. is yours to steward, but in the fullness of time they are all His.

3. What do you need?

Ephesians 2:1 NAS *And you were dead in your trespasses and sins...*

Besides a Savior to prevent you from being eternally separated from God, which He has provided graciously through His son Jesus Christ, what else do you need? What else will put a smile on your face, besides the blood of Jesus? The answer, again, is nothing. IF we really believe what He has done, and that HE has saved us, what else compares to the glory of God dying on our behalf? What is the cherry on the top? What can compare to what He has done?

4. What have you been given?

Ephesians 1:3 *Blessed be the God and Father of our Lord Jesus Christ, who has blessed us with every spiritual blessing in the heavenly places in Christ...*

Eternal life. The Holy Spirit indwelling inside of you. Redemption – Justification – Sanctification - A way home - Eternity with the King - The ability to hear His voice - The gifts of the Spirit - The fruit of the Spirit. Would you trade one of these things in for better circumstances? I know I wouldn't!

Prayer & Application:
As trials and tribulation come this week put any situation up against these four questions and dwell upon what He has done. Set your mind on things above and watch as things below grow so small in comparison to the glory of His awesome love that has already been demonstrated for you!

by **Adam Bower**
Sr. Pastor of Praise Community Church, York, PA & creator of KAIO small groups

Baptism   *

In one of the most famous exchanges in the Bible – The Great Commission – Jesus instructs his disciples to first **baptize**[1] and then **teach**[2] would-be disciples to obey everything that they had learned.

"Therefore go and make disciples of all nations, baptizing them in the name of the Father and of the Son *and* of the Holy Spirit, and teaching them to obey everything I have commanded you. And surely I am with you always, to the very end of the age." **Matthew 28: 19-20**

This language occurs also in Mark, where differentiation is even made about the importance of baptism, "whoever believes and is baptized will be saved, but whoever does not believe will be condemned." **Mark 16:16.** Baptism is a dietary essential for every believer looking to grow and mature. In order to learn, the disciples of the 12 were first baptized; baptism proved to be a precondition for learning.

Both the act and the symbol of baptism are recurrent

conditions for new believers and the teachers directing them to be **established** in salvation and the ***new way*** of going about things, having been transformed and renewed. It's not just vital in doctrine, but vital for becoming a new creation **(2nd Corinthians 5:17)**.

Are you established in this truth? Have you been filled with the Holy Spirit? Have you been baptized with water? Have you been baptized with the Holy Spirit?

Prayerfully consider these questions and ask yourself if they deserve space and time in your prayer life and/or in your "action life."

Prayer: Lord, I thank you that I'm a new creation. That once I emerged from the baptismal waters, I had shed my old, fleshly self. Thanks for your gift of baptism.

Lord, refill me so that I can overflow.

by **Joe D'Orsie**
Communications & Spiritual Life Counsel
Live With Purpose Coaching, LLC

Children of God

*"See what kind of love the Father has given to us that we should be called children of God; and so we are. The reason why the world does not know us is that it did not know him." **I John 3:1 (ESV)***

The world population is estimated now at over 7.2 Billion people. That's a lot of folks. There are 6,900+ unreached people groups. That's 43% of all people groups worldwide totaling nearly 3 Billion People (Joshua Project). An unreached or "under-reached" people is a people group among which there is no indigenous community of believing Christians with adequate numbers and resources to evangelize the rest of the group. These statistics call for action.

We are all God's "children" but not all Children of God (I John 3:9-10). We can't live extensively in both worlds and carry an effective testimony for Christ; but we should live close enough to smell the smoke. God calls us to reach into the fire (the fallen world around us) and deliver the saving message of Jesus Christ. That means we may smell like smoke on occasion. That's a good thing. Not all of us have the opportunity to visit the unreached people groups of the world but we do have the opportunity to reflect our faith daily in the place God has us. Home, work, school, church, with friends. In every situation. It starts with a daily commitment to stay plugged in to the source of life and then love others with the natural outpouring from that source. Our Savior.

Wake up tomorrow morning before your feet hit the ground and ask God to bring an opportunity to tell someone about Jesus today.......that one more or many more may be called Children of God.

Prayer: Father God, it's by your strength and your will that we take another breath. Please help us to reflect who you've made us to be, every day and in every way, your child.

Also see 1st John 3:1-10

by **Steve Adams**
Business/Life Coach & Entrepreneur
Live With Purpose Coaching, LLC

Day 29:

Faith toward God   *

The hallmark verse for faith in the bible is Hebrews 11:1. And although surprisingly cliché in a lot of Christian circles, it's a rarity. Many things in the bible are undefined, at least in human terms, but not the very essence of our call, claim and commission, which is faith. It's actually pointedly defined as the 'substance of things hoped for and the conviction of things unseen.' I believe God knows our inclination of wanting something tangible and that's probably why we have this verse.

"Now faith is the assurance (or substance) of things hoped for, the conviction of things not seen." **Hebrews 11:1 NRSV**

But let's actually seek to understand this verse. How can you be sure of what you're hoping for? How can you be convicted of something you can't see? In plain words, without physical evidence, how can you be certain...that He is who He says He is? This could be answered in some variation of a couple different ways. #1- I can believe He is God because faith isn't a science or a method. And #2- I stand assured in this hope and hold this conviction because, in short, I have faith. It certainly lacks scientific credibility and wouldn't hold up in a worldly court, which is why it has to be faith, devoid of the earthly, human way of comprehending things. It defies logic and the mechanical, proof-seeking mentality of the world. It can't be forced or willed because it's a spiritual posture, not a physical one.

Take a moment to pick apart and ponder Hebrews 11:1 and think of it in a fresh light, as if you hadn't understood it before.

Faith in relation to a balanced diet

"If you put these instructions before the brothers and sisters, you will be a good servant of Christ Jesus, nourished on the words of the faith and of the sound teaching that you have followed." **1st Timothy 4:6 NRSV**

The words of our faith are our nourishment and source for hope and conviction. We're nourished by the faith recorded in scripture and by the testimony of those who trained and inspired us. To be clear, the 'instructions to be put before the brothers and sisters,' as Paul guides Timothy in guarding the faith of his church, are centered in exhortation, encouragement and direction to sustain and replicate faith. It's amazing to see how outward Paul is in exemplifying his faith, that he, throughout his letters to members of the early church like Timothy, is more concerned with the welfare of the church than himself. Without faith in our diets as a staple food, we become starved and begin to turn inward.

Prayer: God, thank you for the simplicity of faith and the Gospel, that it's crystal clear to babes and children, yet distant to analytics and thinkers. Train and tutor me in simple faith, Father, so that I might act in accordance with the movement of your Kingdom.

"Now faith is the assurance (or substance) of things hoped for, the conviction of things not seen." **Hebrews 11:1 NRSV**

by **Joe D'Orsie**
Communications & Spiritual Life Counsel
Live With Purpose Coaching, LLC

Worship

Pure worship is the acceptance and heart attitude that God is God and we are not - *Karl Diffenderfer*

Why do we worship? Some people worship because of what God has done in their lives. They see God impacting their life and have reason to be thankful in their praise to Him. This is an obvious reason to praise God. Unfortunately, life isn't always an amazing mountaintop high. We have valleys in our lives too. We have times of despair, times of wanting selfishly, times of trying to make things go our way.

What if you are hopeless in your circumstances and find no reason to worship? Why would we worship the Lord beyond what He has done for us? How do we praise God in the valleys with greater fervor and Joy than in the peaks?

Well, if you think about it, worshipping him for what He has done for you is very inward focused. I want to challenge you today to think about worshipping God for who He is and not about what He can do for you.

So who is God and why does He deserve worship? Ultimately, it boils down to His supremacy. The potter of all of earth's "clay vessels," who existed before time, longs to be close to you, His child. That's reason for jubilation!

So because God deserves worship, in the valleys as well as the peaks, shall He get it? It depends where you place God in your life. If He is elevated far above your interests and will, then He is in good position to receive your worship. If this order or hierarchy is disrupted, pure worship is not occurring. The higher you view God the greater joy you will experience and the more your soul will leap with praise.

I think we might begin to see the truth of this from Paul and Silas in the **Acts of the Apostles 16:22-25 NLT**

A mob quickly formed against Paul and Silas, and the city officials ordered them stripped and beaten with wooden rods. They were severely beaten, and then they were thrown into prison. The jailer was ordered to make sure they didn't escape. So the jailer put them into the inner dungeon and clamped their feet in the stocks. Around midnight Paul and Silas were praying and singing hymns to God, and the other prisoners were listening.

This story adequately speaks for itself. When we live in surrender and believe in our hearts that God is bigger than any problem we may ever face, then we can worship Him with joy from an attitude of worshipful reverence.

Let me point out two songs that speak to our very souls yet were written in moments of despair. ***It is well with my soul*** and ***Amazing Grace***. If you don't know the stories behind these songs, I would encourage you to look them up and learn about them. They will provide examples of fellow saints who chose to praise the Lord despite their circumstances.

Take-Away: I would urge you to worship God at all times in all things, because He deserves your praise. If you don't feel joy welling up within you to the point where you want to dance and sing as David did, then examine where you're placing God. Is He Kingly, revered and supreme on His throne? Is He Lord over your life and circumstances? Or, does your worship ebb and flow along with your day-to-day whims?

Praise Him today simply for who He is.

by **Karl Diffenderfer**
Business/Life Coach & Entrepreneur
Live With Purpose Coaching, LLC

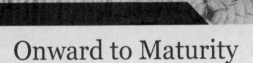

Onward to Maturity

"Therefore let us move beyond the elementary teachings about Christ and be taken forward to maturity, not laying again the foundation..." **Hebrews 6:1**

A simple yet profound little section of this verse is the word "forward." Once we've learned and believed the basics and essentials about this faith, we're then in motion forward, toward something else. That something else is maturity. Maturity doesn't happen overnight to be sure, nor is it typically reported (by those saints that are mature) as being easy, rosy or without challenge. It's certain to include tests, trials, corrections, character developments, moments of weakness, flaming arrows, etc. Satan will always stand in opposition to maturity because it equals the destruction of his kingdom. If we, with the fruit of our lives, are threatening Satan's kingdom, we know we're postured well and are seasoned by the more hearty teachings of Christ which lead to maturity, having moved beyond the basics.

What does maturity look like?

The great thing about attaining or setting out to attain maturity is that we possess the perfect model of what maturity looks like. Jesus personified Christian normalcy and He himself was a good picture of what maturity in the faith looks like. Jesus never wavered on items basic or advanced but His words and deeds spelled maturity for His followers. So what's the main ingredient for arriving at daily maturity?

He only spoke or acted as His father did– **John 5:19/ John 12:49**

"Jesus gave them this answer: "Very truly I tell you, the Son can do nothing by himself; he can do only what he sees his Father doing, because whatever the Father does the Son also does." – **John 5:19**

This means that Jesus' focus was away from himself and toward Heaven. So the long and short of maturity is gravitating toward Heaven with every word, action and breath. The "forward" lean, as we can call it, is a lean that partners with Heaven as opposed to making pacts with the world.

What are some areas that we can put the forward lean into practice?

- Prayer – frequency & fervency
- Obedience – are we acting on what we're commanded to do?

- Bearing good fruit – not simply knowing about maturity but living it

Prayer: Pray today to graduate from the basics and to start walking in the maturity that God has for you. Pray for greater faith in proportion to where He wants to lead you and the assignments He desires to give you. Pray that you're surrounded and encouraged by seasoned believers that can join you in the movement toward maturity.

> *"For I did not speak on my own, but the Father who sent me commanded me to say all that I have spoken." **John 12:49***

by **Joe D'Orsie**
Communications & Spiritual Life Counsel
Live With Purpose Coaching, LLC

Notes:

Notes:

About Live With Purpose Coaching , LLC

Through coaching, counsel, spiritual development, practical tools and other resources, we seek to empower leaders and entrepreneurs to live a life that brings glory to God. Our objective and mission is to inspire business owners, leaders and others to pursue their dreams by intentionally living a life of deep-seated meaning and purpose.

Contact Info

For more information, email us at
info@livewithpurposecoaching.com
or call us at
1 (717)-283-2377

For more resources from the Live With Purpose Team, visit
www.runningdownyourdreams.com

- facebook.com/livewithpurposecoaching
- linkedin.com/company/3574536
- @lwpcoaching
- vimeo.com/livewithpurpose
- www.livewithpurposecoaching.com
- www.livewithpurposecoaching.com/blog

Live With Purpose Coaching, LLC
3113 Main St., Suite A5, Conestoga, PA 17516

More Resources From Our Contributors

Joe Sharp

Running Down Your Dreams – *A 40 Day Journey Focus on Helping you Live a Life of Deeper Purpose and Meaning*

Your Path to Living a Life of Deep Purpose (mini-book)

Pursuing Your Dreams through God's Eyes (Leader's Guide and DVD)

Adam Bower

KAIO – *A Guide to Uncompromising Discipleship* – [Small Group Training Manual]

Brian Connolly

KAIO – *A Guide to Uncompromising Discipleship* – [Small Group Training Manual]

First Dance: *Venturing Deeper Into a Relationship with God*

Awakened: *Coming Awake and Coming Alive Through the Beauty of the Gospel*

Anna Haggard

Mission Drift: *The Unspoken Crisis Facing Leaders, Charities, and Churches*

The Spiritual Danger of Doing Good

Coming Soon...

The Business Revolutionist Mindset – Ravi Kandal & Joe Sharp, with Joe D'Orsie

Running Down Your Dreams [Audio Book] – Joe Sharp & Joe D'Orsie

The Gospel of Inclusion – *How a Cultural Movement is Diminishing Faith and Courting Wickedness* - Joe D'Orsie

Perspectives – Karl Diffenderfer

Made in the USA
San Bernardino, CA
24 June 2015